Christmas Cookies

Kelly Michaels

ISBN-13: 978-1537374765
ISBN-10: 1537374761

"I'm just someone who likes cooking and for whom sharing food is a form of expression."

-Maya Angelou

CONTENTS

Peppermint Dipped Oreos

Servings: 10-12

Ingredients:

1 package Oreos

1 package vanilla candy melts

1 package peppermint baking chips

Crushed soft peppermints

Directions:

1. In a microwave safe bowl, combine the vanilla candy melts and the peppermint baking chips for 3 minutes, stirring every 30 seconds.
2. Dip each Oreo into the melted mixture then sprinkle with crushed peppermints.
3. Let cool on a sheet of wax paper before serving.

Classic Christmas Fudge

Makes 36 squares

Ingredients:

2 cups white sugar

½ cup cocoa

1 cup milk

4 tbsp butter

1 tsp vanilla extract

Directions:

1. Line a 9x9 inch square baking pan with parchment paper and grease.
2. In a medium saucepan, combine the sugar, cocoa, and milk. Stir to mix together well and bring it to a boil while constantly stirring. Reduce heat to low.
3. Cook, without stirring, until a candy thermometer reaches 238 degrees F.
4. Remove from the heat. Add in the butter and vanilla extract. Stir very well with a wooden spoon.
5. Pour the fudge into the prepared pan and let cool for one hour.
6. Place the baking pan in the refrigerator and let set for 3-4 hours.

Snicker Doodles

Makes 2 dozen

Ingredients:

1/2 cup shortening

3/4 cup granulated sugar

1 egg

1 tbsp vanilla

1 1/2 cups all-purpose flour

1/2 tsp baking soda

1/4 tsp cream of tartar

1 tbsp cinnamon

3 tbsp granulated sugar

Directions:

1. Preheat your oven to 350 degrees and line a baking sheet with parchment paper.
2. Cream together the shortening and sugar in a mixing bowl with an electric mixer.
3. Add the egg and vanilla and mix well.
4. In a separate bowl, combine the flour, baking soda, salt, and cream of tartar and mix well.
5. Slowly add the dry ingredients to the wet ingredients.
6. Roll the dough into 1 inch balls.

7. In a small bowl, mix together 1 tbsp of cinnamon and 3 tbsp of sugar.
8. Roll the dough balls into the cinnamon and sugar mixture.
9. Place the balls on the prepared baking sheet and bake for 9-11 minutes or until edges are golden.
10. Let cool on the baking sheet for 5 minutes before transferring to a wire rack to cool completely.

White Chocolate Cranberry Cookies

Makes about 2 dozen

Ingredients:

3/4 cup unsalted butter, at room temperature

3/4 cup brown sugar

1/4 cup granulated sugar

1 large egg, at room temperature

2 tbsp vanilla extract

2 cups all-purpose flour

2 tsp cornstarch

1 tsp baking soda

1/2 tsp salt

3/4 cup white chocolate chips

1/4 cup dried cranberries

Directions:

1. In a large mixing bowl, beat the butter, brown sugar, and granulated sugar with a mixer until smooth and creamy.
2. Add the egg and vanilla and mix together.
3. In a separate bowl, stir together the flour, cornstarch, baking soda, and salt.

4. Slowly mix the flour mixture into the wet mixture until well combined.
5. Stir in the white chocolate chips and dried cranberries.
6. Chill the dough for at least 2 hours.
7. Preheat your oven to 350 degrees F and line a large baking sheet or two with parchment paper.
8. Roll the dough into 1-inch balls and place on the baking sheet(s) 1-2 inches apart.
9. Bake for 8-10 minutes or until golden around the edges.
10. Allow the cookie to cool on the sheet for 5 minutes then transfer to a wire rack to cool.
11. Serve or store in an airtight container.

M&M Cookies

Makes 2 1/2 dozen

Ingredients:

2 ½ cups all-purpose flour

2 tsp cornstarch

3/4 tsp baking powder

1/2 tsp baking soda

1 cup butter

1 cup brown sugar

1/2 cup white sugar

1 large egg

2 tsp vanilla extract

1 11-oz bag M&M's

Directions:

1. Preheat your oven to 375 degrees and line 2 baking sheets with parchment paper.
2. In a mixing bowl, whisk together the flour, cornstarch, baking powder, baking soda, and salt. Set aside.
3. In a separate mixing bowl, mix together the butter and sugar with an electric mixer until creamy.
4. Mix in the egg and the additional egg yolk.
5. Mix in the vanilla.

6. Slowly mix in the flour mixture until combined.
7. Stir in the M&M's with a spoon, reserve 1/4 cup of M&M's for the tops of the cookies.
8. Scoop out 2 tbsp of dough at a time and form into a balls then place on the prepared baking sheet 2 inches apart.
9. Bake for 10-12 minutes until the edges are golden.
10. Allow the cookies to cool on the baking sheet for 5 minutes then transfer to a wire rack to cool completely.

Grinch Cookies

Makes about 3 dozen

Ingredients:

1 box French vanilla cake mix

1/2 cup vegetable oil

2 eggs

2 drops green food coloring

Powdered sugar

Red heart shaped candies

Directions:

1. Preheat your oven to 350 degrees F and line a baking sheet or two with parchment paper.
2. In a large mixing bowl, mix together the cake mix, food coloring, oil, and eggs with an electric mixer.
3. Chill the dough for 30 minutes.
4. Roll the dough into 1-inch balls and place on the prepared baking sheet 1-2 inches apart.
5. Dust each cookie dough ball with powdered sugar and place a heart-shaped candy in the center of each.
6. Bake for 8-9 minutes then let cool on the baking sheets for 5 minutes before transferring to a wire rack to cool completely.
7. Serve or store in an airtight container.

Sugar Cookies

Makes 40-50 cookies

Ingredients:

1 cup unsalted butter, at room temperature

1 1/4 cup sugar

1 egg

1 1/2 tsp vanilla extract

1/2 tsp almond extract

3 cups flour

1 1/2 tsp baking powder

1/4 tsp salt

Colored sugar, sprinkles, or icing-for decorating

Directions:

1. In a large mixing bowl, cream together the butter and sugar until fluffy.
2. Add in the egg, vanilla extract, and almond extract until well combined.
3. In a separate bowl, combine the flour, baking powder, and salt.
4. Slowly add the flour mixture to the butter/sugar mixture and mix well.

5. Roll the dough with a rolling pin between 2 sheets of parchment or wax paper and place on a baking sheet.
6. Refrigerate for 30 minutes.
7. Preheat your oven to 350 degrees F and line 2 baking sheets with parchment paper.
8. Cut the dough into shapes using cookie cutter and transfer to a baking sheet.
9. Sprinkle with colored sugars (if using) and bake for 8-12 minutes.
10. Cool on the baking sheet for 5 minutes then transfer to a rack to cool completely.
11. Store in an airtight container.

Hot Chocolate Cookies

Makes 1 dozen

Ingredients:

1 roll of chocolate chip cookie dough, at room temperature

1 cup Nutella

3 tbsp unsweetened cocoa powder

3/4 tsp ground cinnamon

6 large marshmallows, cut in half

Directions:

1. Preheat your oven to 350 degrees and line two baking sheets with parchment paper.
2. In a large bowl, break up the cookie dough and add the Nutella, cocoa powder, and cinnamon.
3. Beat with an electric mixer until well mixed.
4. Shape the dough into 12 2-inch balls. Flatten the balls and place half of a large marshmallow in the center of each and fold the dough around the marshmallow.
5. Place the balls 2-inches apart on the baking sheets and bake for 10-12 minutes.
6. Cool on the pan for 5 minutes then transfer to a rack to cool completely before serving.

Eggnog Cookies

Makes about 32 cookies

Ingredients:

-Cookies:

2 1/4 cups all-purpose flour

2 tsp baking powder

1/2 tsp salt

1/2 tsp ground nutmeg

1/2 tsp ground cinnamon

3/4 cup butter, at room temperature

1/2 cup sugar

1/2 cup brown sugar

2 large egg yolks

1 tsp vanilla extract

1/2 tsp rum extract

1/2 cup eggnog

-Frosting:

1/2 cup butter

3-5 tbsp eggnog

1/2 tsp rum extract

3 cups powdered sugar

Directions:

1. Preheat your oven to 350 degrees F and line 2 baking sheets with parchment paper.
2. In a mixing bowl, whisk together the flour, baking powder, salt, nutmeg, and cinnamon. Set aside.
3. In a separate mixing bowl, cream together the butter, sugar, and brown sugar until fluffy with an electric mixer.
4. Mix in the egg yolks, one at a time, until just combined.
5. Mix in the vanilla extract, rum extract, and eggnog.
6. Slowly add the dry ingredients to the wet ingredients and mix on low until combined.
7. Scoop tablespoonfuls onto the prepared baking sheets, 2 inches apart.
8. Bake for 11-13 minutes.
9. Let cool on the baking sheets for 5 minutes before transferring to a wire rack to cool completely.
10. For frosting, whip the butter, rum extract, and 3 tbsp eggnog together. Gradually add the powdered sugar. Add additional eggnog until the frosting is desired consistency.
11. Frost the cooled cookies before serving.

Red Velvet Cookies

Makes 2 dozen

Ingredients:

1 box red velvet cake mix

6 tbsp butter, melted

1 cup powdered sugar

1 tsp cornstarch

2 eggs

Directions:

1. Preheat your oven to 375 degrees F and line a baking sheet with parchment paper.
2. Combine the cornstarch and powdered sugar in a small bowl.
3. In a large bowl, combine the cake mix, melted butter, and eggs. Mix on low with an electric mixer.
4. Roll into 1-inch balls and roll in the powdered sugar/cornstarch mixture.
5. Place balls 2-inches apart on the prepared baking sheet.
6. Bake for 9-11 minutes or until set.
7. Let cool on the baking sheets for 5 minutes before transferring to a wire rack to cool completely.

Chewy Molasses Cookies

Makes 36 cookies

Ingredients:

2 cups all-purpose flour

1 ½ tsp baking soda

1 tsp ground cinnamon

½ tsp ground nutmeg

½ tsp salt

1 ½ cups sugar, divided

¾ cups butter, softened

1 large egg

¼ cup molasses

Directions:

1. Preheat your oven to 350 degrees F and line a baking sheet with parchment paper.
2. In a medium bowl, whisk together the flour, baking soda, cinnamon, nutmeg, and salt.
3. In a large mixing bowl, combine the butter and 1 cup of sugar with an electric mixer until light and fluffy.
4. Beat in the egg and molasses until combined.
5. Gradually add in the flour mixture and mix until a dough forms.

6. Roll the dough into 1 inch balls and roll in the remaining ½ cup of sugar.
7. Place the balls on the prepared baking sheet, 2-3 inches apart.
8. Bake for 10-14 minutes or until the edges are firm.
9. Cool for 1 minute on the baking sheet then transfer to a wire rack to cool completely.

Oreo Balls

Servings: 24

Ingredients:

15.5-oz package of Oreos

8 oz of cream cheese, softened

3/4 lb vanilla almond bark, chopped

Christmas colored sprinkles

Directions:

1. Line a baking sheet with parchment paper.
2. Place the Oreos in a food processor and pulse until finely chopped.
3. Place the chopped Oreos in a large bowl and add in the cream cheese. Mix well.
4. Roll the mixture into 24 balls and place on the prepared baking sheet.
5. Place the baking sheet into your refrigerator for at least 30 minutes or until the balls are firm.
6. In a microwave safe bowl, melt the almond bark in the microwave for 2 minutes, stirring every 30 seconds.
7. Place a skewer or toothpick into the Oreo balls and dip into the melted almond bark until coated.
8. Cover the balls with sprinkles and place back onto the baking sheet.
9. Let the balls cool for at least 30 minutes before serving.

Gingerbread Cookies

Makes 24 cookies

Ingredients:

1/2 cup butter, softened

1/2 cup butter flavored shortening

1 1/2 cups sugar

1 egg

1 tbsp vanilla

3 tbsp molasses

3 cups all-purpose flour

2 tbsp baking soda

2 tsp ground cinnamon

1 tsp ground ginger

1/2 tsp ground cloves

1/2 tsp salt

Frosting

Directions:

1. In a large mixing bowl, cream together the butter, shortening, and sugar. Add in the egg, vanilla and molasses and mix well.

2. In a separate bowl, whisk together the flour, baking soda, cinnamon, ginger, ground cloves, and salt.

3. Add the flour mixture to the butter mixture a little bit at a time until it is all mixed in well. It will be thick!

4. Cover and refrigerate the dough for at least 2 hours.

5. Preheat your oven to 375 degrees F.

6. Lightly flour a large cutting board or sheet of wax paper.

7. Roll the dough on the floured surface and roll out into a sheet 1/4 inch thick.

8. Using a gingerbread man (or whatever shape you want!) cookie cutter, cut the dough.

9. Place the cut dough onto a greased baking sheet.

10. Bake for 10-12 minutes.

11. Let the cookies cool then decorate them with frosting.

Peppermint Kiss Cookies

Makes: 2 1/2 dozen

Ingredients:

1 ½ cups powdered sugar

1 1/4 cups butter, softened

1 tsp peppermint extract

1 tsp vanilla extract

1 large egg

3 cups all-purpose flour

1 tsp baking powder

1/2 tsp salt

1/2 cup finely chopped candy cane flavored Hershey's Kisses

Granulated sugar

Additional unwrapped Candy Cane Hershey's Kisses

Directions:

1. Preheat your oven to 350 degrees F and line a baking sheet with parchment paper.
2. In a mixing bowl, mix together the powdered sugar, butter, peppermint extract, vanilla extract, and egg with an electric mixer until creamy.

3. In a separate bowl, whisk together the flour, baking powder, and salt.
4. Slowly add the flour mixture to the sugar/butter mixture until combined.
5. Stir in the chopped Kisses with a spoon.
6. Shape the dough into 1-inch balls and roll in granulated sugar. Place the balls 1-inch apart on the prepared sheet.
7. Bake for 10-12 minutes or until slightly golden.
8. Let the cookies cool for 2-3 minutes on the baking sheet then press a Hershey's Kiss into each cookie.
9. Place the baking sheet in the refrigerator or freezer immediately so that the Kisses don't melt. Leave them in there for 5-10 minutes.
10. Serve or store in an airtight container.

Gingerdoodles

Makes 2 dozen

Ingredients:

1 batch gingersnap dough (see page 19)

1 batch snicker doodle dough (see page 3)

Directions:

1. Preheat your oven to 350 degrees F and line 2 baking sheets with parchment paper and spray with non-stick spray.
2. Prepare the gingersnap dough (see recipe on page 19), roll the dough into 1/2-inch balls, roll in sugar, and set aside.
3. Prepare the snicker doodle dough (see recipe on page 3), roll the dough into 1/2-inch balls, roll in cinnamon and sugar, and set aside.
4. Gently press together a ball of gingersnap dough and a ball of snicker doodle dough and roll into a larger ball. Do this until all the balls are combined.
5. Place the dough balls on the baking sheets, 2 inches apart.
6. Bake for 9-11 minutes. Remove from the oven, let cool on the pans for 5 minutes then transfer to a wire rack to cool completely.

*I halved both of these recipes so I wouldn't have 4 dozen cookies to do something with/eat.

ABOUT THE AUTHOR

Kelly Michaels has been cooking since she could walk. As a child, she would follow her mother around in the kitchen, learning and watching. Her passion has always been food and feeding others. It brings her the most joy in her life. Now she shares her recipes with millions worldwide.

For more recipe books by Kelly Michaels:

Search for "Kelly Michaels Recipes" on Amazon

58031797R00020

Made in the USA
Middletown, DE
18 December 2017